Some True Adventures in the

Life of Hugh Glass,

a Hunter and Trapper
on the Missouri River

Philip St. George Cooke
(1809 –1895)

Reprinted from:
Scenes and Adventures in the Army
Philip St. George Cook
1857

1

SOME INCIDENTS IN THE LIFE OF HUGH GLASS, A HUNTER OF THE MISSOURI RIVER.

THOSE pioneers, who, sixty years ago, as an advanced guard, fought the battles of civilization, for the very love of fighting, may be now recognized in the class of the hero of my sketch, who 1000 miles beyond the last wave of the troublous tide of migration, seek their pleasures in the hunt of a Blackfoot of the Rocky Mountains, a grizzly bear, or a buffalo. It must be difficult to give even a faint idea of the toils and risks of a set of men, so constituted as to love a mode of life only for these attendants; who exist but in the excitement of narrow escapes,—of dangers avoided or overcome; who often, such is their passionate devotion to roving, choose it in preference to comfortable circumstances within the pale of civilization. Little has been reaped from this field, so fertile in novel incident that its real life throws romance into the shade.

The class of people above mentioned, excluded by choice from all intercourse with the world of white men, are at different periods very differently occupied:—at times, as trappers; at others, they live with Indians, conforming in every respect to their mode of life; and often they are found entirely alone, depending upon a rifle, knife, and a few traps, for defence, subsistence, and employment.

A trapping expedition arrived on the hunting grounds is divided into parties of four or five men, which separate for long periods of time; and as the beaver is mostly in the country of hostile Indians, in and beyond the Rocky Mountains, it is an employment of much hazard, and the parties are under great pains for concealment. Trappers, and others who remain in these regions, subsist for years wholly upon game. They never taste bread, nor can they even procure salt, indispensable as it may be considered in civilized life.

To take the beaver requires practice and skill. The trap is set, and then sunk in the stream to a certain depth (when the water is too deep for it to rest upon the bottom) by means of floats attached, and a chain confines it to something fixed or very heavy at the bottom. This depth must be such, that the animal in swimming over it, is caught by the leg. The "*bait*" consists of some strong *scent,* proceeding from a substance placed directly opposite upon the shore; an oil taken from the body of the animal is generally used. The greatest care is necessary to destroy all trace of the presence of the trapper when making his arrangements, which, if discovered by the most sensitive instinct of the animal, it carefully avoids the place; they therefore wade, or use a canoe in setting the trap.

The solitary hunter is found occasionally thus employed, for the sake of the trade with those who visit the country solely for that purpose; getting for his skins the few necessaries of his situation,—blankets, powder, lead, &c.

The white, or more properly, the gray or grizzly bear is, next to the Indian, the greatest enemy the hunter meets with in this region; it is the lion of our forests; the strongest and most formidable of all its animals. It is about 400 pounds in weight; its claws more than three inches long; the buffalo bull, perhaps stronger and more active than the domestic, is a certain victim to its strength. If a grizzly bear is reported to be in the vicinity of an Indian camp or village, fifty or a hundred warriors turn out (as in the East for a lion or tiger) to hunt to its death so dangerous and dreaded a neighbor.

The grizzly bear never avoids, very often attacks a man; while on the other hand, the hunter, but under the most favorable circumstances, carefully avoids him.

In the summer of 1823, immediately after the desertion and conflagration of the Arickara village, consequent upon its attack by the 6th Regiment United States Infantry, a party of eighty men, under the direction of Major Henry (that had volunteered in that engagement), left this point of the Missouri River, intending to gain the head waters of the Yellow Stone to make a fall hunt for beaver. The party had journeyed four days in the prairie; on the fifth we would introduce our hero (who has been rather backward) to the attention of the reader—if, indeed, it has not been already lost in the rugged field prepared for his reception.

On the fifth day, Glass (who was an *engage* in the expedition) left the main body accompanied by two others, to make one of the usual hunts, by which, while subsistence is acquired the party is not detained. Having near night succeeded in killing buffalo, they were directing their common course to a point, near which they knew must be the position of the camp for the night; it was on a small stream, and as they passed near one of its curves, Glass became somewhat detached from the others, intending to drink of its waters; at this moment his progress was arrested by the sight of a grizzly bear issuing from beneath the bank opposite to him. His companions, overcome by their fears, which no obligation to share with him his unavoidable danger could resist, profited by their more favorable situation to attempt escape by flight, leaving him to his destiny.

A contest with a grizzly bear, more tenacious of life than a buffalo, is always dangerous; to insure a probability of success and safety, all the energies must arise in proportion to the magnitude of the danger; and they must be shown in perfect coolness; the slightest falter, which with the many would result from a loss of this presence of mind, would render the case hopeless and insure destruction.

Glass would gladly have retreated, but he knew all attempts would be useless. This desperate situation only nerved him to the combat. All depended upon the success of his first and only shot;—with an aim, cool and deliberate, but quick, lest greater rapidity in the animal should render it more uncertain, he fired his rifle. The shot was a good one; eventually mortal; but its immediate effect was only to raise to its utmost degree, the ferocity of the animal, already greatly excited by the sight and opposition of its intended prey; it bounded forward with a rapidity that could not be eluded, in pursuit of its flying adversary, whom danger, with means of defence, had inspired with deliberate action, but now only gave wings for his flight. But it was unavailing, and he knew it;—an appalling roar of pain and rage, which alone could render pallid a cheek of firmness, chilled him to the soul; he was overtaken, crushed to the earth, and rendered insensible but to thoughts of instant death. The act of contact had been two blows, inflicting ghastly wounds; the claws literally baring of flesh the bones of the shoulder and thigh. Not sated with this work of an instant, the bear continued to pursue, with unabated speed, the flight of the two other hunters:—the chase was to them awfully doubtful:—every muscle of a hunter's frame strained to its utmost tension—the fear of a horrid death— the excitement of exertion—together producing a velocity seldom equalled by bipeds, had been unavailing in contest with that of the superior strength and fleetness of the raging animal. But, fortunately, it could not last; —it was expended in the distance, from loss of blood;— its exertions became more feeble;—the sacrifice of a deserted comrade had saved their lives;—they reached the camp in safety.

When sufficiently recovered, they reported the death of Glass, and their escape from the pursuit of the wounded grizzly bear. A large party was instantly in arms. It had gone but a short distance when the bear was discovered and despatched without difficulty. Glass, they found, was not yet dead; they bore him to the camp, still insensible from the shock of his dreadful wounds. They were considered mortal, but, of course, bound up and treated as well as their circumstances would admit.

A question then arose, how he should be disposed of; to carry him farther was useless, if not impossible; and it was finally settled that he should be left. Eighty dollars were subscribed for any two men who would volunteer to remain with him, await his death, and then overtake the party. A man named Fitzgerald, and a youth of seventeen, accepted the proposals; and the succeeding day the main party continued its route as usual.

For two days they faithfully administered to his wants; then their imaginations began to create difficulties in their situation; at least their inactive stay became very irksome; and as they considered his recovery as hopeless, they equally agreed to think their remaining longer useless. Thus wrought upon, and from innate depravity, they conceived the horrid idea of deserting him, overtaking the party, and reporting his death:—and they determined upon the prompt execution of their design:— nay more, these most heartless of wretches, taking advantage of his first sleep, not contented with the desertion of a sacred trust, robbed him of his rifle, knife, and, in short, everything but a small kettle containing water, and a wallet on which his head rested; and which fortunately contained a razor.

On awakening, how could he realize his situation! Helpless from painful wounds, he lay in the midst of a desert. His prospect was starvation and death. He was deserted by the human race.

But this act, which words cannot sufficiently blacken, perhaps gave a vital excitement. He muttered a mingled curse and prayer:—he had a motive for living! He swore, as if on his grave for an altar, his endless hatred, and if spared, his vengeance on the actors in so foul a deed.

Glass, when his water was exhausted, for fear he should become so weak as to perish for want of it, succeeded with great difficulty in crawling to the edge of the stream, where he lay incapable of further exertion for several days.

Few are aware, until tried, of their capacity for endurance: and the mind seldom shrinks from an exertion that will yield a single ray of hope to illume the darkness of its waste.

Glass did not despair; he had found he could crawl> and he determined to endeavor to reach a spot where he could better hope for succor. He crawled towards the Missouri, moving at the rate of about two miles a day!

He lived upon roots and buffalo berries. On the third day he witnessed near him the destruction of a buffalocalf by wolves;—and here he gave a proof of a cool judgment: he felt certain, that an attempt to drive the wolves from their prey before their hunger was at least somewhat appeased, would be attended with danger; and he concluded to wait till they had devoured about half of it, when he was successful in depriving them of the remainder: and here he remained until it was consumed, resting and perhaps gaining strength. His knees and elbows had, by now, become bare; he detached some of his other clothing, and tied them around these parts, which must necessarily be protected, as it was by their contact with the ground that motion was gained.

The wound on his thigh he could wash; but his shoulder, or back, was in a dreadful condition. For more than forty days he thus crawled on the earth, in accomplishing a five days' journey to the Arickara village. Here he found several Indian dogs still prowling among the ruins; he spent two days in taming one of them sufficiently to get it within his power: he killed it with the razor, and for several days subsisted upon the carcass.

Glass, by this time, though somewhat recovered of the effect of his wounds, was, as may be supposed, greatly reduced; but he continued his weary and distressing progress, upon arms and knees, down the Missouri River. In a few days he was discovered by a small party of Sioux Indians: these acted toward him the part of a good Samaritan. The wound on his back was found in a horrid condition. It had become full of worms. The Indians carefully washed it, and applied an astringent vegetable liquid. He was soon after taken by them to a small trading-house about eighty miles below, at the mouth of the Little Missouri.

GLASS slowly recovered from his wounds. He had been greatly reduced; he was, indeed, when found, a mere skeleton: but a vigorous frame and strong constitution, inured to constant exercise and rough labors, thus rendered iron-like, with little encouragement, quickly recovers from shocks that would be fatal to men of different pursuits. While in this situation, his curse, his oath of vengeance on the authors of half his misfortune, had not been forgotten. When in his feverish dreams he fought his battles o'er,—entrapped the wary beaver,—enticed to its death the *curious* antelope,—when the antlered buck was arrested in his pride by his skill, and weltered before him,—and when the shaggy strength of the untamable buffalo sank beneath his fatal rifle, the bear, the grizzly bear, would still disturb his slumbers; a thousand times would be imaged to his mind the horrid, the threatening grin of its features; now its resistless paw was suspended over his head, with nought to avert the death-inflicting blow—and now its bloody teeth mangled his vitals. And again it would change, and he was confronted by mortal foes;—and he felt a spellbound inactivity: goblin-like they danced before him; retreated, advanced, in mockery of the impotence of their intended victim ;—and then he would see them afar off, with demon countenances of grim satisfaction, in leaving him to a fate they could easily avert, of studied cruelty, worse than death. Awaking with convulsive start, the " Great Nemesis" ever invoked by the unfortunate, would seem to whisper him, " Hast thou forgot thy oath?"

His oath of revenge was far from forgotten. He nourished it as an only consolation; an excitement to hasten recovery. Near two months had elapsed, when Glass was again on his feet. Nor had his ill fate in the least dampened the hunter's ardor: he the rather felt uneasy quickly to resume his adopted habits, which he had so long, so unwillingly foregone.

The pleasures of this roving, independent, this careless life of the hunter, when once tasted with relish, the subject is irreclaimable, and pines in disgust amid the tameness of more quiet occupations.

Glass had found sympathy among his new friends at the trading-house. Who could withhold deep interest from the story of such wrongs? He was destitute of clothing, the rifle, butcher-knife, &c, the means of the support, and even existence of the hunter. These they generously supplied him. A party of six of the *engagees,* headed by one Longevan, had occasion about this time to ascend the Missouri, in a Mackinaw-boat, with the purpose of trading with the Mandans, about 300 miles above; these Glass resolved to accompany; he was anxious to rejoin the trapping expedition from which he had been cut off; a great object, it may be readily conjectured, was to meet the two wretches he was so much indebted to.

The party set out in their Mackinaw in October; and near a month did they tug against the stubborn current of the Missouri: so slow is the progress of all boats but those impelled by resistless steam, that hunters have the greatest leisure to subsist a party thus employed. At the Big Bend, a half hour's walk across reaches the point gained in three days by the boatman's labor. Among the hunters, Glass was, as usual, conspicuous for patience and success. Many fat elk fell by his hand.

The Arickara Indians, driven by armed forces from their extensive village, had retreated up the river to the Mandans for relief. They had been overpowered but not vanquished; and their immemorial hostility to whites was but aggravated to fresh deeds of outrage.

Late in October, the Mackinaw had reached within twenty miles of the Mandan village. Nor had its party been more cautious than is usual on the river. Late in an afternoon, at this time, they unsuspectingly landed to put ashore a hunter; and, as it happened, at a point nearly opposite the spot chosen by the Arickaras for their temporary abode. Ever on the alert, the boatfull of white men had in the morning been descried by one of their out-parties; and a runner had informed the tribe of the glad tidings. So all was in readiness for the destruction of the unconscious objects of savage revenge. Scarce had the boat left the beach, and Glass, as the hunter (his lucky star still prevailing), gained the concealment of willows, when a hundred guns or bows sent forth their fatal missiles, and on the instant rose the shrill cry of war from a hundred mouths. Had a thunderbolt burst from the cloudless heaven upon the heads of the boat's crew, greater could not have been their astonishment, or its destruction. The appalling din was echoed from hill to hill, and rolled far and wide through the dark bottoms; and it was such as to arrest in fear the fierce panther in the act of leaping upon the now trembling deer.

But few guns from the boat sent back defiance to the murderous discharge; the shouts were but answered by the death-cry and expiring groans. The Indians rushed upon their victims, and the war-club and tomahawk finished a work that had been so fearfully begun. They rioted in blood; with horrid grimaces and convulsive action they hewed into fragments the dumb, lifeless bodies; they returned to their camp a moving group of dusky demons, exulting in revenge, besmeared with blood, bearing aloft each a mangled portion of the dead—trophies of brutal success.

Glass had thus far again escaped a cruel fate. He had gained the almost impervious concealment of drifted and matted willows, and undergrowth, when the dread ebullition of triumph and death announced to him the evil he had escaped, and his still imminent peril. Like the hunted fox, he doubled, he turned, ran or crawled, successively gaining the various concealments of the dense bottom to increase his distance from the bloody scene. And such was his success, that he had thought himself nearly safe, when, at a slight opening, he was suddenly faced by a foe. It was an Arickara scout. The discovery was simultaneous, and so close were these wily

woodsmen, that but the one had scarce time
to use a weapon intended for a much greater
distance. The deadly tomahawk of the other
was most readily substituted for the steeled
arrow. At the instant, it flew through the air,
and the rifle was discharged; neither could
see the effect produced, but they rushed into
each other's grasp, either endeavoring to
crush his adversary by the shock of the onset.
But not so the result; the grappling fold of
their arms was so close, that they seemed as
one animal; for a while, doubtful was the
struggle for the mastery; but Glass, not
wholly recovered from his wounds, was
doomed to sink beneath the superior strength
of his adversary, by an irresistible effort of
which, he was rolled upon the earth, the
Indian above. At this instant, the effect of his
unerring shot was developed. The Indian's

last convulsive exertion, so successful, was accompanied by a shout of victory; but dying on his lips, it had marked his spirit's departure. It was as if his fierce soul, sensible of approaching feebleness, had willingly expired in the last desperate effort and the shout of triumph, with which he would have ushered both their souls into the presence of the " Great Spirit."

Redeemed unhoped from death, Glass beheld at his feet his late enemy, not only dead, but already stiffening, with hand instinctively touching the hilt of his knife.

Brief was his breathing-time; he was soon rendered aware that the report of his rifle had been heard by the Arickaras; that his escape was discovered; he had instinctively reloaded his gun, and he renewed a flight of which his life was the stake. Concealment from his pursuers having become impossible, he used his utmost speed in the hope of soon gaining a shelter of such a nature, that he could end a race which could no longer be doubtful. Horses had been called into requisition.

We may suppose his hurried thoughts now turned upon his late narrow escapes, which he feared were of little avail; that the crowning scene was now at hand; or that he prayed that That hand, so often interposed between him and death, would again extend its protection.

Horses were of little aid in 'the thick bottom; but shouts, uttered at occasional glimpses of his form, announced to Glass that his pursuers were thus excited to efforts that could not much longer fail of success; and his thoughts were intensely turned upon some desperate stratagem as his only hope, when a horseman suddenly crossed his path. In his present state of mind, any Indian appeared to his eyes, a blood-seeking enemy. He felt his death now certain, and was determined not to fall single and unavenged; he was prepared for his last mortal strife. But fortune, which apparently delighted to reduce him to the narrowest straits, but to show her freaks in almost miraculous reverses, had thrown in his way a friend. The horseman was a Mandan Indian on a visit to the Arickaras. Attracted by the noise of the pursuit, he had urged his horse's speed to witness the result ; and, coming suddenly upon the object of it, he, at a glance, became aware of the state of the case; a hundred in his place, or he a hundred times to this once, though of a friendly tribe, would have sacrificed the white; but taking one of the sudden and unaccountable resolutions of an Indian, or, perhaps, thinking his interposition of almost impossible avail, at once entered into the excitement of the trial. Be this as it may, he motioned to Glass to mount behind him; it was instantly complied with,—when turning his horse's head, he urged it to its greatest speed. Better ground was soon gained; and avoiding the Arickara camp, they that night entered the Mandan village in triumph.

Here Glass was well received; for the announcement of his presence was naturally accompanied by the recital of his escapes, which nought but the greatest prowess could have accomplished; and nothing is better calculated effectually to engage the interest and admiration of Indians.

And often are acts and events, which are .set down to, the score of fortune or good luck, the result of superiority in qualities immediately conducing to the result. Fortune is not so far removed from the agency of man, that a genius may not, by a happy effort, insure its favor and apparently dictate to fate. A true knowledge of all of Glass's career leaves a first impression on the mind, that it is a rare combination of *fortunate* escapes, of *lucky* accidents; but much of it may be explained as the more natural result of physical strength, cool intrepidity, and untiring patience.

After remaining a few days with the Mandans, Glass, nothing daunted by his past dangers, and equally regardless of new ones, resumed alone and on foot, his journey up the Missouri. The Mandan village is on the left or the northeast bank of the river; it was on the same side he commenced his journey, intending to leave the Missouri at the mouth of the Yellow Stone, about three hundred miles higher up; his object in following watercourses, being to meet with white men, and to run no risk of missing the trapping party under Major Henry, he was so anxious to regain.

His arms were now a rifle, small axe, and the ever necessary knife; his dress, a blanket capote, perhaps a flannel shirt, leather leggins and moccasins and a fur cap: he was, in addition, equipped with a blanket, spare moccasins, and a small kettle, composing a bundle suspended on his back. His route lay through a country infested with the Blackfeet Indians. The Blackfeet muster eight or ten thousand warriors; they live north of this part of the Missouri, and extend west to the mountains; and they are frequently upon the Yellow Stone. To their east live the Assinaboines, Mandans, and Minatarees; to the south the Crows and Sioux; and north and west the Mountain or British Indians. With these tribes they wage perpetual war; and to the whites, incited by British traders, they have been more dangerous than any other Indians. It was through the grounds of this people that Glass had to make his solitary way.

The country on the Missouri, from the L'eau qui-court up, is nearly bare of timber; the river bottoms are narrow, and on but one side at a time, changing at intervals of twenty or thirty miles, and sometimes there are none at all, the ground being generally high bluff prairies. This open, bare country is at times, as far as vision extends, in every direction blackened with buffalo; it is within bounds to say, that a hundred thousand may be seen at a glance. One of these vast herds, all taking the same course to cross the Missouri, detained Glass for two days, declining the perilous attempt to penetrate a mass, which, when in quick motion, is as irresistible as the waves of the ocean.

In two weeks he reached the mouth of the Yellow Stone, having met neither white man or Indian; here he crossed the Missouri on a raft made of two logs tied together with bark, and continued his journey up the Yellow Stone. This is a wide and shallow stream, emptying into the Missouri from the south; it is even more muddy and rapid than the latter river, to which it is believed to have considerable agency in imparting these qualities.

It was more than three hundred miles to the forks of the river, nearer than which he could scarcely hope to meet with any of the party, since it had set in very cold, which would cause the small detachment of trappers to be drawn into that point, where he knew they were to winter. Right weary did he become of his journey, inured as he was to the toils and dangers which surrounded him. Almost in despair, and having at times nearly resolved to retrace his steps and winter with some of the most friendly Indians, one morning in December he was overjoyed to discover a hunting party of white men. On reaching them, long was it before they could make up their minds to believe their eyes; to believe that it was the same Glass before them, whom they left, as they thought, dying of wounds, and whose expected death was related to them by two witnesses. It was to them a mystery; and belief of the act of black treachery, which could only explain a part of it, was slow in being enforced upon their minds. Overwhelmed with questions or demands of explanation, it was long before he could ascertain from them in return, that the party had rendezvoused for winter at the Forks, which was but a few miles distant; that Fitzgerald was not there, having deserted; and that the youth was still one of the expedition.

Fiercely excited with conflicting feelings,—the escape of the main object of his just revenge,—chiefly for which he had made so long a pilgrimage,—and the certainty of soon facing the accomplice of his crime, Glass hastened to enter the encampment.

Nearly the first person he met, was the unfortunate and guilty young man; and it so happened they came upon each other suddenly. All attempt must fail to describe the effect of his appearance upon the youth. Had he awoke from a deep sleep in the embrace of a grizzly bear, or been confronted at noonday by the threatening ghost (and such he believed of him) of a deeply injured enemy, greater could not have been his fear. He stood without power of any motion; his eyes rolled wildly in their sockets; his teeth chattered, and a clammy sweat rose upon his ashy features. Glass was unprepared for such a spectacle; and well was it calculated to create pity; for some moments he could not find words, much less the act of his purpose.

He leaned upon his rifle; his thoughts took a sudden turn; the more guilty object of his revenge had escaped; the pitiful being before him was perhaps but the unwilling and over-persuaded accomplice of his much elder companion;—these, and other thoughts crowded upon his mind, and he determined upon the revenge which sinks deepest upon minds not wholly depraved, and of which the magnanimous are alone capable; he determined to spare his life.

With dignity and severity, but great feeling, he thus addressed the petrified youth, who but expected immediate death: "Young man, it is Glass that is before you; the same that, not content with leaving, you thought, to a cruel death upon the prairie, you robbed, helpless as he was, of his rifle, his knife, of all with which he could hope to defend, or save himself from famishing in the desert. In case I had died, you left me to a despair worse than death, with no being to close my eyes. I swore an oath that I would be revenged on you, and the wretch who was with you; and I ever thought to have kept it. For this meeting I have made a long journey. But I cannot take your life; I see you repent; you have nothing to fear from me; go—you are free—for your youth I forgive you." But he remained mute and motionless; his reprieve, or rather pardon, for such it must be considered in a country where the law has never reached, could scarcely allay the awe and fear of an upbraiding conscience. He was taken off by some of the witnesses of the scene, in whose breasts pity had begun to take the place of wonder and resentment.

Glass was welcomed as one recovered from the dead; one whose memory—such is our lot—had already been swept far upon the gulf of oblivion. His services, ever highly appreciated, were again engaged in the company, where we leave him, employed as the rest, in the sole labors of supplying provisions, and of self-defence from the extreme coldness of the winter. Only adding, that his determination of revenge upon the more worthy object of punishment from his hands, far from being abated, was rather confirmed; and that, what he considered a sacred duty to himself, though postponed to a more convenient season, was still nourished as a ruling passion.